LISSETTE DORSEY, RN

Wear Your Hat with Excellence

Nurse's Pocketbook

First published by Zees Ink Press 2020

Copyright © 2020 by Lissette Dorsey, RN

First edition

ISBN: 978-0-9989362-3-9

Cover art by Lastenia Worrell

*This book was professionally typeset on Reedsy.
Find out more at reedsy.com*

This handbook is dedicated to all nurses.

Your good work doesn't go unseen.

Contents

Introduction	ii
A Modern Nightingale Pledge	v
Center Yourself	1
The Right Attitude	3
Positivity	5
Problem Solver	6
Leadership	8
Nurse (noun)	10
About the Author	12

Introduction

Nursing is a rewarding profession that is a privilege to serve others in need.

As nurses we are allowed to care for people in whatever capacity that is needed; mentally, physically, emotionally and spiritually.

As we care for patients or clients, we deal with the whole patient; that is our primary focus.

This is the uniqueness of nursing because we are right in the center with the patient.

As nurses, we assess, plan, and set goals to evaluate, advocate, teach, counsel and coordinate care.

Nursing theorist Imogene King states, "The goal of nursing is to help individuals and groups attain, maintain and restore health" (King, 1981, p. 5).

Depending on the level of care the patient needs, it can become very stressful.

Nurses wear many hats to ensure patient care has been

achieved.

While caring for patients we collaborate with allied disciplines of the health care team; to provide excellent care and a great outcome for the patient.

Because nurses are the main connection to the patient, juggling coordination of care and communication with the healthcare team can be stressful.

It is especially stressful when conflict arises.

As nurses navigate through the day, we must be equipped to deal with the demands and pressures of the job.

It is very easy to lose sight of the top priority. Although the issues that come up are important and need to be addressed, this must be achieved professionally.

In my experience I have learned that if you keep the patient as the top priority when conflict or pressures arise, your actions will allow you to have a patient based perspective that will keep you focused on how to proceed.

Nurses are not robots, we have personal challenges in our lives as well.

I'll share what got me through those tough days: being centered, having the right attitude, having a positive outlook, creating a problem solving mindset and developing leadership.

This is the main reason for this handbook, to provide nurses with simple tips that lead to a productive and successful day.

"Nurses are at the heart of healthcare."
Donna Wilk Cardillo

* * *

A Modern Nightingale Pledge

I pledge myself here, before my God and in the presence of this assembly, to practice my profession with integrity.

I will endeavor to maintain and elevate the standard of nursing, both as a science and as an art.

I wholeheartedly recognize the importance of high standards of care and of personal accountability.

I devote myself to the healing, protection, and welfare of those committed to my care.

I accept a duty to work for the improvement of health in the communities in which I live and work.

I will hold in confidence all personal matters committed to my keeping, and will respect the privacy of medical information.

I will act with compassion in ethical matters.

I will not knowingly administer or consume any harmful substance.

I commit to interdisciplinary collaboration and lifelong learning.

I fully acknowledge the seriousness of the responsibility that I accept in my calling, and the significance of this pledge that I take today.

Lorita Renfro, BSN, RN

* * *

Center Yourself

Center yourself mentally before you get to work. Participate in an activity that settles your mind to a place of peace, calmness and reassurance that everything will be okay; because you are in control.

This can be achieved through prayer, meditation, exercise, etc. Being centered brings an alignment of power that will allow you to focus and not be easily distracted or irritated with issues that come with the job and everyday life.

The more we practice and become consistent with centering ourselves, the more we are in control of our day.

This allows us to stay positive throughout our day, looking at issues that arise with optimism and confidence. This gives us the ability to problem-solve.

A great part of nursing is problem-solving. To effectively execute excellent care, nurses must be in the right frame of mind. Self-care not only has personal benefits but also may help nurses to role model desirable self-care behaviors to others.

> "Maybe this one moment,
> with this one person is the very reason
> we're here on earth at this time."
> Jean Watson.

* * *

The Right Attitude

Come to work with the right attitude. This is a crucial part of having a successful workday.

Being self-aware, being centered and understanding ourselves will help us to understand others and improve interaction.

When we can be honest about our biases and expectations, our approach will be more effective.

The right attitude will allow us to build trust with patients and colleagues; and in turn enhancing team-building.

As nurses, we will face challenges in this area based on conflict in the work environment.

Examples of work environment conflict can include poor leadership, favoritism, low morale, staffing issues and not being heard.

Nurses are resilient. We always find a way to make it through the day. Ending your day successfully will have better results.

Having the right attitude puts things in perspective leading to better decisions which bring about great outcomes and change.

"The character of the nurse is as important as the knowledge she possesses."
Carolyn Javis

* * *

Positivity

As nurses, we could find a million reasons for negativity as we go through our day. Anywhere from staffing shortage to lack of supplies. I could go on and on. One thing is clear that becoming negative will not end your day well. Being overwhelmed can easily shut down your mind and have you responding from a place of negative emotion. Negativity leads to closed doors while positivity leads to open doors. A new policy can result from approaching a bad situation with positivity. Coming from a place of resolution brings better work conditions.

> "Sometimes I inspire my patients.
> Most often they inspire me."
> Unknown.

* * *

Problem Solver

For nurses, problem-solving makes a world of a difference for patients, co-workers and the entire team.

I have witnessed how nurses develop this capability rather quickly.

Due to our constant interaction with the health care team and the system of the institution in which we are employed, we can quickly connect the dots.

Nurses can allow our creativity to bloom with new ideas or refine old ones.

We have the ability to assess, evaluate and problem-solve with knowledge and confidence.

Continuing education such as advanced degrees, certifications, journal subscriptions and workshops keeps nurses up to date with the latest knowledge necessary for them to function at their best.

Everyone wins when nurses are allowed to build upon their knowledge and skills.

"Let us never consider ourselves finished
nurses...we must be learning all of our lives."
Florence Nightingale.

* * *

Leadership

Every nurse is a leader! Nurses lead the care of their patients. Leadership in nursing makes a tremendous difference in patient care and patient experience.

Through my personal professional experience, nurses that are leaders possess certain characteristics and have always left an indelible mark on those around them.

A few characteristics of effective leadership consist of kindness, compassion, knowledge, effective communication skills, the ability to inspire those around you and having a visionary perspective.

As nurses, we bring a wealth of knowledge, compassion and skills to the healthcare industry.

Never forget the impact we make in people's lives every day. As nurses sometimes we are disappointed when we are not recognized for our hard work.

Fortunately our true recognition comes from God and

lies in the joy our patients receive when they are cared for with kindness, compassion, and love.

> "Do not wait for a leader...
> Look in the mirror, it's you."
> Katherine Miracle.

* * *

Nurse (noun)

nurse

noun

1: a person who cares for the sick or infirm
   specifically **:** a licensed health-care professional who practices independently or is supervised by a physician, surgeon, or dentist and who is skilled in promoting and maintaining health.

Merriam-Webster

* * *

Spanish - enfermera
Russian - medsestra
Irish - altra
Polish - pielęgniarka
Chinese - hùshi
Korean - ganhosa
Arabic - mumarada
Igbo - nọọsụ
Yoruba - nọọsi
Filipino - nars
Haitian - enfimyè

* * *

About the Author

Lissette Dorsey is a Registered Nurse. Her nursing career spans over 20 years of experience in various areas of the healthcare spectrum.

Her nursing experience consists of hospital and community based settings.

She began her career as an LPN primarily working with the elderly in nursing homes.

She progressed to a hospital setting as an RN, where she developed a strong foundation in Med-Surg.

She later branched into procedure areas such as TEE

(Transesophageal echocardiogram), EP (electrophysi-ology), IR (interventional radiology) and PIRR (post interventional recovery).

She has also worked in the community as a visiting nurse and IV infusionist.

Her current position is staff nurse in ambulatory services out-patient.

She is currently in pursuit of completing her BSN. After-ward, her plans are to pursue an MSN in holistic nursing.